71 Absolutely No Prep TEFL Games and Activities:

The Book for Smart ESL/EFL Teachers Who Like to Save Time!

Jackie Bolen

www.eslactivity.org

Table of Contents

About the Author: Jackie Bolen

I taught English in South Korea for a decade to every level and type of student, including every age from kindergarten kids to adults. These days, I'm living in Vancouver and teaching English to a variety of students. In my spare time, you can usually find me outside surfing, biking, hiking or on the hunt for the most delicious kimchi I can find.

In case you were wondering what my academic qualifications are, I hold a Master of Arts in Psychology. During my time in Korea, I completed both the Cambridge CELTA and DELTA certification programs. With the combination of years teaching ESL/EFL learners of all ages and levels, and the more formal teaching qualifications I've obtained, I have a solid foundation on which to offer teaching advice. I truly hope that you find this book useful and would love it if you sent me an email with any questions or feedback that you might have (jb.business.online@gmail.com).

Jackie Bolen around the Internet

ESL Speaking (www.eslspeaking.org)

YouTube (https://www.youtube.com/c/jackiebolen)

Instagram (www.instagram.com/jackie.bolen)

Pinterest (www.pinterest.com/eslspeaking)

If you can't get enough ESL games, activities, and other useful stuff for the classroom in this book, you can get even more goodness delivered straight to your inbox every week. I promise to respect your privacy—your name and email address will never be shared with anyone for any reason. Sign-up here.

Introduction to the Book

I love to make learning English fun and interesting for my students. Happy, engaged students will remember the content far better than bored, disinterested ones! That's why I've written this book—to give other teachers some fun ideas to try out with their students. The best part is that all of the 71 games or activities require essentially nothing in the way of preparation or materials.

Quite honestly, this is the book that I wish I'd had when I first started teaching. There just wasn't anything like this 20 years ago. Instead, I relied on *Dave's ESL Cafe* for some ideas for my classes, but it was quite difficult to find something that would work. I usually ended up making my own games instead.

Skip over the frustration and use this book! You'll find 71 TEFL games and activity ideas that will ensure a great class. You should be able to find one that'll work for whatever you're teaching in just a minute or two. These games have been tried and tested over my teaching career and the result is things that work, in the real world—your classroom!

What this book isn't meant to do is replace a textbook. The games are not a comprehensive treatment of the English language. Instead, if you teach conversation or general English, I recommend using an appropriate textbook (I like "Let's Go" for children, and "4 Corners," "Smart Choice," "World Link," and "Touchstone" for adults).

Then, supplement the lesson from the textbook with one or two of these fun games. Perhaps use one as a warm-up activity at the beginning and then another as a review activity at the end. Finally, you can find some "just for fun" activities that are ideal if you teach at a summer or winter camp, or just want to have a "party" day in class.

I hope this will be your go-to resource for all things "no prep time required" ESL games and activities! There are a variety of activities that will work well for larger classes of 20+ students. All of them will work for smaller classes of 4-12 students. And many of them are ideal for private tutoring or online teaching as well. Many of them are based on pair work but in this case, the teacher can act as the partner for the student.

6

The activities are organized into levels (all levels, lower-level students, and higher-level students. Each activity lists the skills needed (speaking, listening, etc.) and the time required to complete it.

A quick note on materials I'm assuming that all students have a pen/pencil and paper and that the teacher has a whiteboard or smart board of some kind.

Games and Activities for All Levels

3 Things

Skills: Writing/listening

Time: 10+ minutes

Have students think of three random things for a partner. They should be objects, animals or people of some kind.

Then, students have to write a story using all three of these things. It can be silly, and actually, the sillier the better! The length of the story and the time you give depends on the level of students. Students can share their story with the person who thought of the three objects.

For beginners, you may want to do this together as a class. Students could shout out three random words and then you can write them on the board. Then, they could help you write a simple story using those words. Or, consider showing students an example of a simple, silly story using random words and then have them make their own using new words but with many of the same sentences from the example one.

Procedure:

1. Put students into pairs and each person has to think of three random objects for their partner.

2. Students have to write a short story using those three objects. Consider using an adaptation (mentioned above) for beginners.

3. Then, they can share their story with their partner. You can also ask for volunteers to share their stories with the class or require that students turn in a more polished version of this for a homework assignment.

Dictation

Skills: Writing/listening

Time: 5-10 minutes

Dictation is an excellent way for students to practice their listening and writing skills. Say a sentence out loud, and students have to write it down, using the correct spelling and punctuation.

To level up the difficulty, if students write down a question, get them to answer it (and vice versa for statements). For example:

- What did you do last night? (students answer the question: I watched TV last night)

- I'm thirteen years old. (students make a question: How old are you?)

Procedure:

1. The teacher says a statement or question, and students have to write it down in their notebooks.

2. (Optional) Students answer the question, or make a question for a statement.

Find Something in Common

Skills: Speaking/listening

Time: 10-15 minutes

This activity is an excellent way for everyone to get to know each other. The students stand up with a piece of paper and pencil in their hand. They have to talk to everyone in the class to try to find something in common (they are both from Seoul, or they both know how to play the piano). Once they find this thing in common, they write it down along with the person's name. Keep going until most of the students have talked to everyone.

Teaching Tips:

This is a great activity for students to practice the sub-skill of initiating a conversation, which is something that many of them find quite difficult. Coach students before the activity starts and give them a few phrases or conversation starters to keep in their head if they get stuck. However, since this game is mostly for higher level students, I wouldn't write them on the board because students will be referring back to them throughout the activity when they are capable of remembering a few phrases in their head and can recall them easily.

Many students struggle with speaking because it happens in real time. Unlike in writing, where we can plan first and then produce later, in speaking, planning and production overlap and often happen at the same time. If our students focus too much on planning, fluency can suffer. If they focus too much on production, accuracy can suffer. In this activity, fluency is far more important than accuracy because the students are having short, small-talk type conversations. I tell my students not too worry too much about choosing the perfect vocabulary word, or exact grammar constructions, but instead just focus on communicating quickly, in a way that is "good enough."

Tell students that while it is okay to have short conversations about the thing they have in common, the goal of the activity is to try to talk to most of the people in the class, so they need to keep moving and talking to new people. I recommend to my students that they try to spend only 1-2 minutes talking with each person.

Procedure:

1. Students stand up with a pencil and paper in their hands.
2. They talk to another student and try to find something they have in common by asking some questions. Questions that work well are ones like, "Have you ever _____ (lived abroad)?", "Are you _____ (an only child)?" or, "Do you _____ (have a brother)?"
3. Once they find something in common, they write that down, along with the person's name.
4. Then, they find a new partner and continue until they've talked to everybody in the class or the time is up.

Finish the Sentence

Skills: Listening/writing

Time: 5-10 minutes

This is a simple activity that can be used for any grammar point that you're teaching. It's partly listening/dictation practice and partly a writing activity.

Think of a few sentence starters. Or, use it as a review activity for things covered in previous classes. For example:

"If I were you, _____."

"Despite the cool weather, _____."

"I wish he/she _____."

Say the sentence starter out loud, and students have to write them down. Then, give students time to finish the sentences in a grammatically correct way. As you can see, they lend themselves to any and all grammatical constructions.

As the students are finishing their sentences, circulate throughout the class offering assistance and correcting errors. If you have a very large class and are unable to offer personal assistance to each student, you could have them submit it for a homework assignment.

Round off the activity by eliciting one or two examples for each sentence starter.

Procedure:

1. Think of some sentence starters related to your target grammar.

2. Dictate them one by one to students who write them down in their notebooks.

3. Students finish the sentences in a grammatically correct way. Monitor for errors and offer assistance if required. Elicit some examples to share with the class to finish off the activity.

I'm an Alien

Skills: Speaking/listening

Time: 5 minutes

Students have to describe something to an alien who doesn't know about life on Earth.

Tell students that you are an alien. Then, get them to explain what they know about the topic of the day. It's ideal for those very common units in ESL textbooks like the weather, sports, hobbies, food, TV, etc.

Encourage students to give as many details as possible. This is ideal for helping students to activate their prior knowledge about a topic before jumping into the rest of the lesson. It can give you some clues about what students already know and what they don't.

Teaching Tip:

Have some fun with this! I use my photoshop skills to put my face onto the body of an alien and put it into the screen to start it off.

This activity is ideal for private teaching. It'll help to ensure that you're not teaching the student things he or she already knows well.

Procedure:

1. Pretend that you're an alien and don't know anything about a certain topic.
2. Have students explain everything they know about that topic.
3. Continue on with the lesson. You now know what students know, and what they don't about the topic.

Only 1 Question

Skills: Listening/speaking

Time: 10-20 minutes

Students have to think of one single question about a certain topic. For example, if you're teaching about holidays, they could use any of the following:

- What's your least favorite holiday?

- What did you do last _____?

- What do you think about Valentine's Day?

There are many possibilities but I usually make a couple rules that it must be interesting and also that it can't be a yes/no question. Once students have done this, they ask at least 10 people their question and quickly record their answers with 1 or 2 words. After the time is up, they tabulate the answers and can quickly report to a small group what they found out about the topic. You can ask each small group to share the most interesting thing they learned with the entire class.

Procedure:

1. Give students a topic and have each student make one *interesting* question about it. Give them examples of interesting versus boring questions.

2. Each student talks to 10+ students, using the same question. They quickly write down answers with 1-2 words.

3. Students tabulate the results and report them to a small group of 4-6 people (or the entire class if fewer than 10 students).

Phone Show and Tell

Skills: Speaking/listening

Time: 10-15 minutes

In small groups, each person chooses one image on their phone to share with the group. They should show the image and discuss what's happening and why they chose to share it.

Teaching Tip:

An easy way to quickly change groups is to number students, for example, 1 to 4. When you change groups, tell all 1's to get together, 2's together and so on. Be sure to show each new group where to sit. If you have ten groups, you can simply divide the new groups in half.

Procedure:

1. Optional: in advance, prepare a PPT of an image from your phone.
2. Divide students into groups of 3-5 and ensure that any students who don't have a phone are divided evenly among the groups.
3. Show the PPT and tell students that it is a picture from your phone. Discuss the picture; tell what is happening and why you chose to share that particular picture.
4. Instruct them to take out their own phones and give them 2-3 minutes to choose a photo to share with their group.
5. If you want to extend the activity, you can have students change groups and repeat the activity, either with the same image or after choosing a new one to share.

Picture Dictation

Skills: Listening/speaking

Time: 15-20 minutes

This is the ultimate no-prep activity. It is great to do with beginner students learning prepositions. Students will need a piece of notebook paper, a pencil, and a book or file folder to use as a barrier.

To begin the activity, students each draw a picture which they do not allow anyone else to see. Working in pairs, students will take turns describing their picture while their partner draws what is described to them. The speaker can repeat what they've said and answer any questions, but they can't show their picture to their partner. When both partners are finished dictating and drawing, they can compare the original to the copy.

To extend to activity, you can have the students work in groups of three or four, rather than pairs. Additionally, the pairs/groups can share their drawings with the class and the class can vote on which drawing most closely matches the original.

Teaching Tips:

You may want to write some vocabulary items on the white board or post some flash cards as inspiration. You may also want to set some guidelines for minimum or maximum number of items in the drawing, as well as a time limit for the activity. Remind students throughout how many more minutes they have to complete their drawing. "5 minutes left, 3 minutes left, last minute!"

This can work with any size class, but you may need to use a classroom noise app, if your class is large and the students don't use "inside voices" well. The lower the students' language level, the more you will need to circulate around the class monitoring their language choices, making corrections as needed.

Procedure:

1. To demonstrate, have students take out paper and pencil. Describe a simple picture and have them draw what they hear. Then, show your picture to the class.

2. Divide the class into pairs and have students take out fresh paper and a file folder or book to use as a barrier, so their partner can't see.

3. Have them each draw a picture. You may want to give a time limit and/or post words or flash cards on the board as inspiration.

4. Have students play rock-scissors-paper to determine who goes first. The winner will describe their picture and their partner will draw what they hear.

5. Students should be encouraged to ask as many questions as they wish in order to replicate the drawing without looking at it.

6. When that student is finished, they switch roles.

7. When both students are finished, they compare the original and dictated drawings.

Question of the Day

Skills: Speaking/listening

Time: 5 minutes

Ask a question to spark a short student discussion. Current events, new movies, etc. are good topics to get people speaking in English for a few minutes at the beginning of class. If there is a new blockbuster out, that will be of interest to most students. The ones who have seen it can briefly summarize and answer the other students' questions about it.

Procedure:

1. Begin class by asking students how they have been and if anything interesting has been happening lately.

2. Use one of the students' answers as a segue to a current events question, such as, "You saw _____ last weekend? Who else saw that? What happened?" Just pick a movie, sporting event, or other topic that the majority of students are likely to have seen or at least know.

Retell the Story 1-2-3

Skills: Speaking/listening

Time: 15-20 minutes

This is a fluency activity which can be done with beginners by having them introduce themselves. Higher level students can tell a story they know or recap a story that was covered in class. Give the students a bit of time to think about what they're going to say; the lower the level of students, the more time they will need.

Working in pairs, each student will tell the same story three times. The first time, they will each speak for one minute. Then, have the students switch partners. With their second partner, each person will tell the same story, but add more detail, so they speak for two minutes. Again, everyone will switch partners. The third time they tell their story, everyone should speak for three minutes.

You might need to reduce these times for beginner students if they are struggling to keep talking. With an advanced class, you might want to reverse the order to 3-2-1, in order to help them focus on retelling only the most important parts of the story and working on fluency.

Teaching Tip:

An orderly way to have students quickly switch partners for this activity is to have only half of the students move. If students sit in rows, have even numbered rows move up one seat. If students sit in blocks of four, number the students 1-2-3-4, and instruct which numbers to switch seats.

Procedure:

1. The teacher can do a demonstration, telling either a story or introducing themselves.

2. Divide students into pairs after giving them a minute or two to think of a story to tell.

3. Tell students which partner will go first (i.e.: students on the right) and start the timer for one minute. When time is up, start the timer for the second partner.

4. Instruct the students who spoke first to move to the seat in front of theirs (or according to your classroom configuration), set the timer for two minutes, and complete round two.

5. After both partners have had a turn, have the same students move again, set the timer for three minutes, and complete round three.

The Hot Seat

Skills: Speaking/listening

Time: 3-4 minutes/student

This is a great activity with small classes of no more than 10 students. Each student has to think of one interesting thing about themselves that they want to share with the class. My examples are that I have an identical twin and that my mom is also one (it's really true!), or that I've been to more than 50 countries. Then one by one, students have a chance to sit in the "hot-seat." They say their interesting statement and the class has to quickly ask five follow-up questions. The best thing about this activity is that there are usually a lot more questions that students want to ask and they'll follow up during the breaks or after class.

Procedure:

1. Each student thinks of one interesting thing about themselves.

2. The first student comes to the front of the class, sits in the "hot-seat," and says their interesting statement.

3. The class has to quickly ask them five follow-up questions, to which the student answers, and then the student goes to sit back down in their regular seat.

4. The next student comes up and the procedure is repeated until all students have been in the "hot-seat."

Toilet Paper Icebreaker

Skills: Speaking/listening

Time: 5-10 minutes

This is an icebreaker activity for the first day of class that can help students get to know each other in a fun way. Bring in a roll of toilet paper, and depending on the size of your class, tell the students they can take a certain number of pieces (4-7 works well). You can also play this game with a bag of wrapped candies (wrapped for sanitary reasons) and as the student completes each speaking task, they can eat the candy. In fact, maybe all your classes would like this option better but it depends on your budget! Don't give them any other information.

Once everyone has their papers, explain that they have to tell the class one thing about themselves for each square of paper they have. For each sentence, they "throw-away" one square until they're done. If you have an extremely large class, you can put the students in groups of 5-6 for this activity instead of playing all together as you would for a smaller class.

Teaching Tip:

Students are always so curious about why they have a choice for how many they chose. Be mysterious and don't give away the secret until everyone has chosen.

Procedure:

1. Divide the students into groups of 5-6 (larger classes), or play together for a smaller class.

2. Students choose the number of pieces of toilet paper that they want depending on your minimum and maximum criteria.

3. Tell students that for each square they took, they must say one interesting thing about themselves.

4. The first student says one thing about themselves and discards that square into the pile in the middle (or eats the candy!). The other students could make a response of some sort such as "Me too," or "Really?", or "I can't believe it!" The second student

says one thing and discards a square. Continue in a circle until all squares are used up.

5. An optional, but fun variation for higher level students is that they can have a chance to ask a follow-up question after each statement, but only one and the fastest person gets to do it. For each follow-up question, they can discard a square into the pile.

Words in Words

Skills: Writing

Time: 5-10 minutes

You probably did this when you were in school. Give students a word and have them make as many words as possible using the letters in that word. For example: "vacation" = a, on, no, act, action, taco, ant, van, etc. Ggive a point for each word, so that the student with the most words wins, or give more points for longer words. When time is up (about five minutes), show students the possible answers.

Wordles.com has a tool that allows you to type in a word and get the possible words. For vacation, they listed 45 words, some of which I should have thought of myself and some of which are "Scrabble words." Since students will not possibly know all of these words, it is up to you whether you show all the answers or an abridged list.

Procedure:

1. In advance, prepare a long word and write it on the whiteboard or a PowerPoint or give students individual worksheets.

2. Give students a time limit of five minutes to make words from the letters in the word.

3. To make it a competition, when time is up, give students points for each word and you may wish to give bonus points for longer words.

4. When the activity is finished, show students all of the possible words they could have made. Find them at www.wordles.com.

Would You Rather?

Skills: Speaking/listening

Time: 5 minutes

Make 1-5 "Would you rather _____?" questions. You can also get the students to help you come up with them. For beginners, keep in mind the limited vocabulary range. Students can share their ideas about which option is preferable to them.

Put students into pairs and have them discuss some, "Would you rather?" questions. They can be positive (Would you rather go to the beach or forest for a vacation?), or negative (Would you rather die by drowning or in a fire?).

For lower-level students, I usually do this activity with the entire class. I start off by asking students a question (beach or forest vacation, for example). Then, I have students put up their hands to vote. After that, I elicit some reasons why from the students.

Teaching Tip:

This activity is very adaptable to just about any level, depending on the questions that you choose. It's also a nice option for private teaching or online classes because the teacher can discuss the questions with the student.

Procedure:

1. Make some simple, "Would you rather _____ or _____?" questions.
2. Students can also help you make the questions.
3. In pairs, small groups, or with the entire class, students can discuss their answers.

Word Association

Skills: Reading/writing/listening/speaking

Time: 5 minutes

To introduce a new vocabulary word, write it in the middle of the board or paper and have students take turns adding as many words or images related to that word as possible. For large classes, have students work in groups with separate pieces of paper taped to the wall or the top of the table/grouped desks. After a given amount of time (2-3 minutes, or when you see no one is adding anything new), discuss their answers.

Teaching Tips:

For large classes, butcher paper works best because more students can write at one time. If that isn't possible, have 5-6 board markers available.

If using butcher paper (or A3 in a pinch), prepare in advance by taping it to the wall unless students will be working at their desks. If students will be working at their desks, write the word on each table's page in advance, but don't hand them out, until you have given your instructions.

Procedure:

1. Write a single new vocabulary word on the whiteboard or butcher paper.
2. Have students take turns adding as many words or images related to that word as possible.
3. After 2-3 minutes (or less, if no one is adding anything new), discuss their answers.

Games and Activities for Lower-Level Students

Alphabet Game

Skill: Writing

Time: 5 minutes

This is a simple way to introduce a topic. Some examples include jobs, cities, or animals. Have pairs of students write down A~Z on a piece of paper. Give them 2-4 minutes to think of one word per letter of the alphabet that falls within the category (e.g. animals).

Here's an example of what students should NOT do:

A. alligator, ant, antelope

I make a rule that students can't use proper nouns. If you want to increase the difficulty or if you have a small class, you can make a rule that if two teams have the same word it doesn't count. This forces students to think more creatively, but it's too time-consuming to check this for bigger classes.

Example: Topic = animals

A. alligator

B. bat

C. cat

Etc.

At the end, you can ask students to count how many words they got (remember only one for each letter). Then, check the top 1-3 teams, depending on how many prizes you have to give out! Or, if you have a very small class, you could easily check all the lists.

Procedure:

1. In pairs, students write down the alphabet on a piece of paper.

2. Give students a topic and a certain amount of time.

3. Students think of one word per alphabet letter about the topic. Check who has the most letters completed at the end of the allotted time. Option for small classes: don't count repeated words so students have to think more creatively.

Categories

Skills: Speaking/listening/writing

Time: 5 minutes

Students can review by brainstorming words they know in a given category, such as food, job, hobbies, etc. It's a nice way for students to activate prior knowledge they may have about a topic.

Variation 1 (Writing): Students work in small groups of 3-4, making a list of all the words they can think of for that category. The group with the longest list wins.

Variation 2 (Speaking): State the category (jobs). Students take turns adding one word at a time to the list (teacher, engineer, driver, etc.). If a student repeats a word or says a word which doesn't fit, they are out. This variation is better suited to small classes or groups working independently. It also doesn't require anything in terms of materials, unlike variation 1 which does require pen and paper.

Procedure:

1. Begin by dividing students into groups of 3-5. Small classes can work as a whole.

2. For a speaking & listening activity, have students take turns adding a word related to a certain category by saying it out loud. If students can't add a word that's not a repeat of what's already been said, they are out.

3. For a written activity, give a time limit of around three minutes to brainstorm and write as many words that match the category as possible. The group with the most correct words wins.

Chain Spelling

Skills: Speaking/listening

Time: 5 minutes

Have all the students stand up and the teacher says a word. The first student says the first letter, the next student the next letter, and so on until the word is done. Then, say a new word.

If someone makes a mistake, they sit down and you start with the next student and new word. Continue until you have only 1 or 2 students standing. This is an excellent "filler" game if you have a few minutes left-over at the end of class—just use whatever vocabulary you were teaching that day.

Teaching Tip:

Spelling is an often neglected skill in many classrooms but it's an important one. When I taught academic writing at a major university in South Korea some students had atrocious spelling which hampered their ability to write well. Nobody will take you seriously, no matter how good your ideas are, if you make basic spelling mistakes. That's why I try to include at least a little bit of it into my classes.

Procedure:

1. All students stand up.

2. The teacher says a word.

3. The first student must say the first letter.

4. The next student must say the second letter, etc.

5. If incorrect, the student has to sit down. The teacher says a new word and the game continues until there are only one or two students remaining.

Disappearing Words

Skills: Reading

Time: 10 minutes

      This vocabulary game is an easy way to force students to keep a set of new vocabulary words in their heads, or to review past words. Write down 10-15 words on the whiteboard and give students 1-2 minutes to study them. Then, if you have a big class, ask everyone to close their eyes as you choose one or two words to erase. Students open their eyes and have to tell you what is missing and where it was. If you have a small class, you can choose individual students to close their eyes and then tell you the missing word(s) after you've erased them. You can either write those words in their spots again or add new words to the mix and continue the game.

Procedure:

1. Write down 10-15 vocabulary words on the whiteboard.

2. Have student(s) close their eyes as you erase 1-2 words.

3. Students open their eyes and tell you which words are missing and where they were.

4. You can write those same words back in, or add new words to the mix in those same spots and continue the game.

Flashcard Sentences

Skills: Speaking

Time: 5-10 minutes

Use this for whatever grammar and vocab points you're teaching. The only materials you need are a pile of flashcards.

Go around the room asking each student or pair a question. Pull a flashcard from your pile and then the student has to make a sentence using the grammar point with that card. A correct sentence gets the card; not correct, and the card goes back at the bottom of the pile. The winner is the person or the team with the most points.

Teaching Tip:

This works best in small classes of eight or less. If you have bigger classes, it's possible to put students in groups of four and have two teams of two competing against each other. You can act as the referee if required.

Procedure:

1. Get a flashcard from your pile.
2. Ask one student or pair to make a sentence with that card.
3. If correct, the student keeps the card.
4. If incorrect, the flashcard goes to the bottom of the pile. Continue until the cards are gone or the time is up.

Flyswatter (Verb Review)

Skills: Listening/reading

Time: 5-10 minutes

To review verb usage in a fun way, this is your activity! Think of some sentences that require different conjugations of verbs.

Write a bunch of verbs that the students know randomly on the whiteboard. The verbs shouldn't be conjugated but are just in base form. For example: eat/go/play/see/teach.

Put students into teams. The first student from each team comes to the front. Give them each a flyswatter.

Start the sentence but don't include the verb. For example, "Last night, he ____." The first student to swat a verb is given a chance to make a sentence. If she chose "eat," she could say, "Last night, he ate pizza." It's correct so she'd get a point for her team.

If incorrect, the other student gets a chance to make a sentence with the same verb. If both are incorrect, nobody gets a point. Use the same question again later in the game, give the class the correct answer, or get the rest of the class to shout out the correct one. Continue the game until all students have had a chance to play.

Either erase the word that the student slaps and put in a new one, or just leave them as is. I prefer to erase the word in most cases, except for total beginners who may find this game a bit challenging already.

Procedure:

1. Prepare a list of sentence starters.

2. Write various verbs (not conjugated) on a whiteboard.

3. Divide students into two teams.

4. One student from each team comes up to the front. Give them each a flyswatter.

5. Say the beginning of the sentence. Whoever slaps a verb first has a chance to make a sentence with what you've said and the verb they've chosen. It should be correct in both form and meaning. If correct, they get a point. If incorrect, the other student has a chance. Continue until all students have had 1-2 chances to play.

Give a Reason

Skill: Writing

Time: 5-10 minutes

To review conjunctions, try out this simple activity. Write some sentence starters on the board using "because." For example:

- I was late for school because _____.

- My mom was angry at my sister because _____.

- I failed the test because _____.

Put students into pairs and they have to think of the most creative reasons they can to finish off the sentences. Compare answers as a class and choose the most interesting ones.

Teaching Tip:

This activity lends itself well to "so" sentences as well that deal with consequences. For example:

- I missed my bus so _____.

- I woke up late so _____.

Procedure:

1. Write some sentences on the board with "because," but leave the reason blank.

2. Put students into pairs and they have to give the reason to finish the sentence.

In Front of/Behind/Between

Skills: Listening/speaking

Time: 5-10 minutes

Place some flashcards on your board ledge or leaning against the wall at the front of the room. I like to use three sets of three. Place them so that the students can't see the pictures, but show them what is on the flashcards before you place them. Arrange them so that there is one card in front, one in between and one behind.

Then, ask some questions such as, "What's in front of the elephant?" or "What's between the giraffe and the gorilla?" The students that can answer the question correctly get a point. I require that students answer the questions in full sentences.

Teaching Tip:

It's easy to adjust the level in this game. To make it easier, reduce the number of flashcards in play. To make it harder, increase the numbers of flashcards and also the variety of questions you ask by including "next to/beside" or "under" and "over/above" if you place some of them in a stack on the table.

Procedure:

1. Place flashcards in three stacks of three on the blackboard ledge or leaning against a wall, so that students can't see the pictures. But, make sure you show the pictures as you are facing them.

2. Choose one student (or a pair) and ask a question. For example, "Where's the elephant?" Students will have to answer, "It's between the monkey and hippo."

3. If correct, the student gets one point.

Is that Sentence Correct?

Skills: Reading/writing or speaking

Time: 5 minutes

This is a sneaky way to get students to make grammatically correct sentences using target vocabulary and also work on their listening skills at the same time. Write down some sentences which may or may not have an incorrect element in it.

Elicit some opinions from the students about whether or not they think the sentence you said is correct or not. If incorrect, get the students to tell you why. Continue on with a few more sentences. Alternatively, students can write down the correct sentences in their notebook.

It's also possible to do this activity in a bit more student-centered way. In this case, put students into pairs or groups of three. Get students to read a sentence and then talk about whether or not it's correct and what they'd change about it. Then, elicit some answers from the class once students have already talked about it with their group.

Procedure:

1. Say a sentence that may have an incorrect element in it.

2. Students have to say if the sentence is correct or not.

3. If incorrect, students have to say what's incorrect and what they'd change.

Last Person Standing

Skills: Speaking/listening

Time: 5-10 minutes

Choose a topic based on whatever you're teaching. Some examples are jobs, food, animals, and things in the kitchen or classroom. Have the students stand up in a circle. Clap your hands in a beat 1-2-3 and say a word related to that topic on the third beat. Continue the 1-2-3 rhythm and have the next person in the circle say a different word related to the topic on the next third beat.

If students repeat a word, or don't have one, they must sit down and the game continues with the remaining players. The game finishes when there is one person left standing.

Procedure:

1. Have students stand in a circle and assign a topic.

2. Clap your hands in a 1-2-3 beat and say the first word related to the topic on the third beat.

3. Continue the rhythm and have the next student say a different word related to the topic on the next third beat. If students repeat a word or don't have one, they must sit down.

4. The game continues until there is one person left standing.

Line Up

Skill: Listening

Time: 5-10 minutes

Line up is a quick activity that you can use as an icebreaker, or just about any time for that matter! Students can stand up. Then, give them a criterion by which they have to organize themselves in a straight line. Some examples:

–   Oldest to youngest

–   Tallest to shortest

–   Highest number of people they live with to the fewest

–   Number of pets (most to least)

Students can do this by talking (only in English!), or by using hand gestures.

Teaching Tip:

Be sure to make it clear which side of the line is for which, or it can get pretty chaotic. For example, if you're doing birthday month, be sure to point to the right and say, "January" and then point to the left and say, "December."

Procedure:

1. Students stand up.

2. Give students a criterion by which they must organize themselves into a line.

3. Students organize themselves (with, or without talking).

4. The teacher can check if students are in the correct place by asking how old each person is along the line.

Memory Circle

Skills: Listening/speaking

Time: 5-10 minutes

This is a game that I often use in classes with a maximum of ten students. It requires students to listen very carefully to what their classmates are saying because they'll be required to repeat it.

To set it up, make a rule about what kind of words or grammar that students can use. For example: animals or past tense. Adjust the rules and criteria according to the level and age of students. It's best to make it challenging, but not impossible so that everyone can have a chance to play at least once in a round. I'll use past tense for my example.

Everyone will stand up, in a circle, and I start the game off, "I ate pizza." The next student says, "She ate pizza, and I studied English." The next student says, "She ate pizza, he studied English, and I watched TV." And so on it goes, around the circle. If someone forgets someone or gets it incorrect, they are out and have to sit down. I usually let it go until there are 2-3 people left and then I give them a prize of some sort and start over with a new set of criteria.

If you have very low level students, a single word works better. For example, they can say "Cat," "Cat and dog," or "Cat, dog, and fish."

Teaching Tip:

Participate in the game as well to impress students with your memory skills. It's a good way to end the game if it's taking too long—take a final turn and then declare the game finished!

Procedure:

1. Assign a topic or grammar point.

2. All the students stand up in a circle.

3. The first student says a word related to the topic.

4. The next student repeats the first word and adds a new word.

5. The third student repeats the first two words and adds a new one, etc.

6. If students miss a word, they sit down and are out of the game.

Me, Too!

Skills: Speaking/listening

Time: 10 minutes

This is a simple activity to uncover what students have in common with one another. If possible, arrange the seats in a circle, so everyone can see each other. Begin by sharing a fact about yourself that you don't think is unique or unusual. For example, "I like to hike in my free time."

Any students in the class who also enjoy hiking should stand (or raise their hands) and say, "Me, too!" Go around the circle and have each student share one fact about themselves related to what you just said. For example, "I like to hike at ABC park."

Extend the activity by keeping track of numbers and noting which facts are common to the most students.

Teaching Tips:

Remind students that these are not unusual facts; these should be things they expect to have in common with at least one other person.

Procedure:

1. If possible, arrange the seats in a circle.

2. Begin by sharing a fact about yourself that you don't think is unique or unusual. For example, "I like to hike in my free time."

3. Ask any students in the class who also enjoy hiking to stand (or raise their hands) and say, "Me, too!"

4. Go around the circle and have each student share one fact about themselves.

5. Extend the activity by keeping track of numbers and noting which facts are common to the greatest number of students.

My World

Skills: Writing/reading/speaking/listening

Time: 10-15 minutes

This is an icebreaker activity that you can do on the first day of class to introduce yourself and then have the students get to know one or two of their classmates. Start by drawing a big circle on the whiteboard with the title, "My World." Inside the circle there are various words, pictures or numbers that have some meaning to you.

For example, inside my circle there might be 1979, blue, 67, a picture of two cats, and a mountain. The students would then have to make some guesses about why these things are special to me. The correct answers are: my birth year, favorite color, number of countries I've been to, my pets, and hiking which is my favorite hobby.

Teaching Tips:

This is a good activity to practice some functional language dealing with correct or incorrect guesses. Teach students how to say things like, "You're close," "Almost," "You got it," "That's right," and "Really? No!"

Remember that the goal of our classes should be to make them more student-centered than teacher-centered, so try to minimize the amount of time that it takes for students to guess what's in your circle. Most of them are quite easy with only one or two more difficult ones. Then, if required, give students some hints so they are able to get the harder ones. To increase student talking time, it's always better to have students playing this activity with each other instead of only with you.

For beginners, this activity might be a bit of challenge. Write these question forms on the whiteboard:

- Is this your _____ (hobby, birth year, age, favorite color)?

- Do you have */a/an _____ (cat, three family members, etc.)?

- Have you _____ (visited, gone to, tried, etc.)?

Procedure:

1. Draw a big circle on the board and write "My World" at the top. Put in some words, pictures or numbers inside the circle that have some meaning to you.

2. Have students guess what each thing means. Give hints if necessary.

3. Students prepare their own "world." I usually give students around five minutes to do this.

4. Students can play with a partner or in small groups of 3-4. Have students work in pairs or small groups to correctly arrange the sentences, or words within the sentences.

Name Five Things

Skills: Listening/writing

Time: 5 minutes

This is an excellent warm-up activity to review vocabulary words from the previous class. Put students into pairs. They'll need one piece of paper and one pen. Tell them to name five _____. The category will depend on the level and age of students.

For beginners, do easy things like animals, colors, fruits, etc. For higher level students, use more difficult. For example, things that move, animals with four legs, things that can fly, breakfast foods, etc.

The first team to write down their five things raises their hands. Check to make sure all the answers are appropriate. To save time, I usually only check the answers of the team that finishes first, although you could easily check all the answers in smaller classes.

Procedure:

1. Put students into pairs with one piece of paper and one pencil.

2. Tell the class to name five _____. Each team has to write down five words on their paper.

3. Once a team is finished, they raise their hands.

4. Check to make sure the first team's answers are appropriate. Optional: Check all the answers from every team if you have a small class of fewer than ten students.

Odd One Out

Skills: Reading/speaking or writing

Time: 5 minutes

Use Odd One Out to review vocabulary from the previous classes, or just to have some fun with English vocabulary. Write up a few sets of vocabulary words on the whiteboard. I use four in one group, with one of them being the odd one out. For example: orange, cucumber, apple, banana. Cucumber is the odd one out because it's not a fruit.

Procedure:

1. Make 4-6 groups of four words, with one of them being unlike the others.

2. Put students in pairs and have them choose the odd word from each group and also write (or say) why they chose it. For example: Cucumber—not a fruit.

Pass and Ask

Skills: Speaking/listening

Time: 10-20 minutes

Pass and Ask is a simple activity that helps student work on questions and answers. Use any classroom object like a whiteboard marker or pen. Start the game off by holding the marker. Ask a question and then pass it to the person who has to answer it.

There are two variations to this activity. The first one is that the person who answers the question has to ask a question and then pass the marker on. My rule is that it can't be the same question that was just given.

The second variation is that the person who answers the question can pass the marker to someone else who must think of a question.

If you have a class of fewer than ten students, play it all together and there will be enough student talking time. However, for bigger classes, break the class down into smaller groups of 6-10. Circulate around the class monitoring each group.

Procedure:

1. Find a classroom object like a whiteboard marker. Think of a question and ask it to one student. Pass the marker to them and they have to answer it.

2. That student thinks of another question and passes the marker to the person who has to answer it. Or, they pass the marker to someone else who has to ask a question.

3. Continue until everyone has had a chance to play. This is a quick activity that takes around 30 seconds per student per round. You can play 2-3 rounds if students are having fun with it.

Role-plays

Skills: Writing/reading/speaking/listening

Time: 20-40 minutes

Partner role-plays are an excellent way to get students practicing using new vocabulary in a real-life context. Give the students a conversation starter to get them going. For example, if you're talking about *feelings* in class that day, you can use:

A: Hey _____, how are you doing?

B: I'm great, how are you?

A: I'm _____ (sad, embarrassed, angry, bored, etc.). ***Anything besides, "I'm fine, thank you, and you?" is good. ***

B: Oh? What's wrong?

A: _____.

B: _____.

Another context that I often use this activity with is *illness or injury*. For example:

A: Hey _____, you don't look (sound) so good! What's wrong?

B: Oh yeah, I'm not good. I _____.

A: Really? _____.

B: _____.

A: _____.

One final context that I use this with is *excuses*. For example:

A: Hey _____, you're _____ minutes late!

B: I'm really sorry. I've been/I had to _____.

A: Hmmm . . . _____.

Give the students about ten minutes to write the conversation with their partner. You can adjust the number of lines and how detailed of a starter you give to suit the ability level of students. For lower-level students, it can be helpful to have a word bank relevant to the context on the whiteboard so that the writing portion of this activity doesn't get too long (you can also provide them with a detailed, fill-in-the-blank script).

Then, students memorize can their conversation (no papers when speaking!), and do a role-play in front of their classmates if you have a small class of fewer than ten. Remember that you should try to maximize the amount of time students are talking. If you have a larger class, there are a few different ways to handle this. You could get pairs to come up to your desk and show you their conversation while the other students are working on something else, you could use it as a speaking test of some kind, each pair could join with one or two other groups and perform for them, or finally you could have students make a video of themselves and send you the link or upload it to *YouTube.*

I like this activity because it's perfect for lower-level students who want to practice "conversation" but don't quite have the skills to do this on their own, and it's also a good way to force your advanced students to use some new grammar or vocabulary that you're teaching.

Teaching Tips:

Having students make conversations is very useful for practicing functional language and speaking sub-skills. I usually choose one or two functions to mention when I'm giving the instructions for the activity and provide a bit of coaching and language input surrounding that, depending on the level—beginners will need more help.

The functions that fit particularly well with partner conversations include agreeing, disagreeing, apologizing, and asking advice. The sub-skills that you can emphasize are things like turn-taking, initiating a conversation, speaking for an appropriate length of time, stress and intonation, responding (really?), and cohesive devices, particularly noun pronoun reference: A: I saw a movie last night. B: Which one did you see? A. I saw Iron Man. It was good.

This is one of the most useful things you can do in your conversation classes, especially for beginner or intermediate students so make sure you try it out at least once or twice over the course of a semester. It gives students a chance to have a real conversation which will build a lot of confidence but they won't have the pressure of coming up with something to say on the spot. That said, it gets boring if you do this every class; I generally do it about once a month for a class that meets twice a week over the course of a semester.

Procedure:

1. Prepare a conversation starter.

2. (Optional) Pre-teach some language that students could use, if you haven't done that already in your lesson.

3. Write the conversation starter on the whiteboard.

4. Have students complete the conversation in pairs. Then, they must prepare to speak by memorizing and adding in stress and intonation. You could give some individual help to each pair to assist them in knowing what to stress and how to do it.

5. Have students stand up and "perform" their conversation if you have a small class. In larger classes, there are a few other options (see above).

6. Reward teams for interesting conversations, good acting (no reading), and correct use of grammar/vocabulary that you were teaching that day.

Sentence Substitution Ladder

Skills: Speaking/listening/(writing optional)

Time: 5-20 minutes

This is a simple activity to get students to think about how they can use the words they know. They will be very familiar with substitution drills, but this goes a step further to get lower level students comfortable with using the language a bit more creatively. They have the knowledge, but they may need a push to use it.

Write a simple sentence on the whiteboard. Then, instruct the students to change one word at a time to make a new sentence. Each position must be changed one time (first word, second word, etc.), but it doesn't have to be done in order.

Student can do this by writing new sentences in their notebook (3-5 is a good number to aim for). Or, students can do it by speaking with a partner, or you can do it together as an entire class by getting ideas from the students and then writing the sentences on the whiteboard.

An example ladder would be:

Original sentence: I saw a black cat walk under a ladder.

- I saw an orange cat walk under a ladder.

- We saw an orange cat walk under a ladder.

- We saw an orange cat run under a ladder.

- We saw an orange cat run under the bed.

- We saw an orange cat run to the bed.

- We heard an orange cat run to the bed.

- We heard an orange dog run to the bed.

Procedure:

1. Write down a simple sentence on the board.
2. Have students change one word at a time to make a new sentence.

45

Spelling Bee

Skills: Listening/speaking

Time: 20+ minutes

Have you seen a spelling bee in-person or on TV before? They are surprisingly exciting! Consider having one in your own class. It's ideal because it can take up a large amount of time but requires nothing in the way of preparation.

You can prepare a list of words beforehand or think of them off the top of your head. I like to make a list because the students think it's fairer if they're getting the next word on a list, instead of something you thought of specifically for them. If planning this at the last minute, it's easy enough to prepare a short word list in just 1-2 minutes.

Procedure:

1. Make a list of appropriate vocabulary words (or think of them off the top of your head). If you're using a textbook, flip back to the chapters you've covered recently as a nice place to start.

2. Divide the class into two or more teams. Say the first word to the first student and they have to spell it.

3. If correct, they get a point for their team. If incorrect, ask the first student from the next team.

4. Continue until the allotted time is up, or each student has had a turn. It generally takes around 30 seconds per student per round. However, you could play as many rounds as you'd like to. Or, you could play until one team has a certain number of points.

Spelling Challenge

Skills: Listening/writing

Time: 10 minutes

Try out this fun spelling game. Divide the class up into two teams. If you have a larger class, and more whiteboard space, consider 3 or 4 teams to make it more student-centered. One student from each team comes to the whiteboard and is given a marker.

Say a word and the students have to race to spell it correctly. The first student to do this gets a point for their team. Continue with different words until all students have had a chance to play.

If you have a minute or two, make a list of words beforehand. If you're using a textbook, flip back to the units you've covered and it'll take no time at all. It's also possible to think of words off the top of your head. For beginners, things like numbers, animals, colors, days of the week or months work well.

Procedure:

1. Divide the class into two teams (or more).

2. One student from each team comes up to the whiteboard and takes a marker.

3. Say a word and each student has to write it on the board. The first student to do it correctly gets a point for their team.

4. Continue until each student has had a chance to play 1-2 times.

Telephone

Skills: Listening/speaking

Time: 5-10 minutes

Everyone has played telephone before. Students line up in two or more rows (teams) starting from the front and going to the back. The student at the front of each team is given a sentence. Consider the level of the students carefully when choosing your sentence—make sure the first students on each team can all understand it easily.

It can work well to take something that you've been teaching from the textbook and adjust it slightly. They whisper the sentence one time to the next student. That student whispers it to the person in front of them, etc. The last person to hear the sentence must correctly state what they have heard.

The team with the closest phrase is the winner. It some cases, the teacher might have to explicitly forbid students from using their L1. This is usually obvious if the ending sentence has the same meaning as the original but uses synonyms.

Teaching Tips:

All teams can have the same sentence or you can give each a different one. I sometimes like to take the heads of each team into the hall, give each a different sentence and allow them the chance to have me model the pronunciation before we begin. Then, the students return together and the game begins.

Keep the teams to about 8-10 students or fewer in order to increase speaking time. Remember that students will only say one sentence each per round. Remind students that even if they didn't hear the sentence clearly, they need to make their best guess and tell *something* to the next person instead of nothing.

Procedure:

1. Divide students into teams, unless you have a very small class and can play with everyone together. Larger teams will make for funnier results.

2. Have the teams stand in line, starting from the front to the back.

3. Have the first students from each team join you in the hall. Give each a sentence to repeat and return together when each is satisfied they know what to say—and how to pronounce the words. Or, you can whisper the same sentence once to each person at the front of the line.

4. The students whisper the sentence once to the next person, who whispers it to the next person and so on.

5. The last student in each line says the sentence they heard.

6. The group with the sentence closest to the original wins.

Vocabulary Pictionary

Skills: Speaking/listening

Time: 10-20 minutes

This a great review game with no prep required. Divide students into teams and choose which team will go first. That team will choose a representative to go to the white board and they will have to draw pictures (I use a pile of flashcards) that their team guesses. The goal is to get as many points as possible in a specified amount of time (2 minutes). Then, the next team does the same thing. You can play as many rounds as you wish.

I've done this with classes of up to 40 students and it has worked well, as long as no one got too rowdy. In those large classes, students sat at tables, rather than individual desks, so were able to work together easily. If you have a large class seated at desks, you should arrange them into groups of 4-8 desks, depending on class size. When I have done this in classes of ten or fewer, I divide them into two teams.

Procedure:

1. Divide students into equal teams of 4-8. Have each team choose a representative to draw.

2. Demonstrate by drawing a picture representing a familiar term on the white board and elicit guesses from the students.

3. The team that correctly guesses the word will go first. The other team representatives will play rock-scissor-paper to determine their order.

4. Have the drawer from the first team go to the board and show them a flashcard. They have to draw it.

5. As they draw, their team guesses the correct word. The drawer takes another card and their team continues to guess. Continue until the specified time is up.

6. Continue until each team has had at least one chance to play.

What's That Called?

Skill: Writing/reading

Time: 5-10 minutes

If you're teaching about classroom vocabulary, then try out this fun activity. Give each student a few Post-It notes and have them walk around the classroom, labelling common objects (clock, chair, textbook, table, etc.). Students will have a pen or pencil in their hand so emphasize that it's walking only and it's not a race to see who can get the most objects!

When you run out of Post-It notes, or most things are labelled, have students sit down. Then, walk around the class and review students' labels to ensure they're correct. Pick them up as you go.

When you have all the labels, mix them up and redistribute them back to the students who must put the labels on the objects as a kind of review.

Procedure:

1. Give each student a few Post-It notes. They will take their pencil and walk around the class, labelling the objects.

2. When they're done, check and see if their labels are correct. Collect the papers as you go.

3. Redistribute the papers back to the students who must put the labels on the objects one more time.

What's the Question?

Skill: Writing/listening

Time: 10 minutes

This is a fun whiteboard game that you can play with everyone but very advanced students (it will be too easy for them). Put students into two, three or four teams. The number of teams will depend on the size of your class and whiteboard, but the more teams the better. A greater number of teams is more student-centered, but you'll have to have a larger whiteboard because everyone needs space to write on it.

Then, say the answer to some question. The difficulty depends on the general level of the class. Students have to write a possible question that corresponds with your answer. The first person to do it gets a point for their team. Continue the game until everyone has had a chance, or the time is up.

Here are some beginner examples, with a possible answer in brackets:

- My name is Jackie. (What's your name?)

- It's sunny. (How's the weather?)

- It's behind me. (Where's the clock?)

Note that there may be more than one answer for some questions. You will have to use your discretion.

Procedure:

1. Put students into teams and have one student from each come up to the whiteboard.

2. Say an answer to a question and students race to see who can write the question first.

3. The first person who is correct gets a point for their team.

4. Continue until everyone has had a chance to play.

Games and Activities for Higher-Level Students

2 Truths and a Lie

Skills: Writing/listening/speaking

Time: 20-30 minutes

Try out this nice icebreaker activity. Play in groups of four. My general rule is with minimal or no follow-up questions, it takes around three minutes per student. However, if you allow two minutes of follow-up questions, it takes about six minutes per student. You'll also want to allow a couple of minutes for students to think of their three statements.

Students write three sentences, one of which is false. They read their sentences and the other students in the grup guess the false one. Higher level classes can ask three questions or question the person for a pre-determined amount of time (two minutes) to determine the false one. A correct guess gets one point. Each student gets a turn to play.

Teaching Tips:

This is a useful activity for practicing the speaking sub-skills of initiating a conversation and responding to something in a questioning way. For example, students might say, "So you can make/play/do _____? I kind of don't believe you! Tell me _____" if you allow question or response time.

You can do this as a single activity in one class or do it over a series of classes/days. For example, I taught a winter camp where I had the same group of students for ten days in a row. My class had twenty students, so as a warm-up for each day, two students had to go in the "hot-seat" (one at a time) and we got to ask the students questions about their two truths and one lie for three minutes. I appointed a "captain" to keep track of the points throughout the two weeks. The two winners got a $5 *Starbucks* gift certificate, which was a small way to add some *friendly* competition to the class.

Give points to the student in the hot-seat for anyone who doesn't figure out the correct answer. But, either do this style of game play or the other way I mentioned above.

If you do both, it gets complicated and confusing very quickly!

Emphasize that students must pick things that are "big picture" ideas. The terrible examples I give are things like birthdays, hospital they were born in, name of sister, etc. There is simply no way to verify this information through asking any sort of interesting questions. Better categories are things like hobbies, travel, part-time jobs, skills and abilities. I have students write down their statements and try to catch any of the bad ones before the game starts. Of course, they shouldn't indicate whether they are true or false when you're checking them so that you can play too!

Procedure:

1. Write three sentences on the board about yourself: two are true and one is not. Or, just say your three sentences slowly out loud.

2. Explain to students that they are to do the same for themselves.

3. Do your demonstration with one group. Say your sentences and those students can ask three questions (or have two minutes) to ask questions.

4. Each student in the group must choose for themselves which sentence is false at the end of that time. Reveal the answer and whoever guessed correctly gets a point.

5. Each student gets a chance to share their three statements and the same procedure is followed.

Or, the students can play the game in small groups, making sure that each person gets a chance to share their three statements. Help to facilitate this by acting as timekeeper for the entire class by saying things like:

- Start! Share your three statements.

- Two minutes of question time.

- Please vote on the false statement.

5-Minute Debate

Skills: Speaking/listening

Time: 10 minutes

Give students an age-appropriate controversial statement. If you are knowledgeable about pop culture, start with, "so and so is the best X (singer, soccer player, whatever)," if students are too young for truly controversial topics. In pairs or small groups, have them debate the sides. Assign sides, if too many agree or disagree with your premise.

Scaffold this activity with language like, "I think _____ because _____." "I agree with X, but _____."

Procedure:

1. Divide students into pairs or small groups.

2. Give students a controversial statement. Something in the news recently may make a nice option.

3. Give students a time limit to discuss the merits of their side, trying to change the mind of their "opponent".

4. If necessary, begin with some helpful language, such as, "I feel _____ because _____."

5. Finish with a quick poll to see if anyone changed their mind on the topic.

5 Senses

Skills: Writing

Time: 5 minutes/round

This activity is a fun way to help students work on descriptive writing. Bring in an object to class like a piece of chocolate or a carrot. It should be something that you can eat in order to do the "taste" sense. In groups, students have to write down a few descriptive words for each sense (see, smell, feel, hear, taste). Obviously, "hear" will not be easy for a carrot, but you could tell students to think about what happens when you snap a carrot in half.

When the time is up, each group can share 2-3 of their most interesting words with the class. You can also do this activity with another object if you wish. It works well as a daily warm-up in a writing class, if you bring in something different each day.

Procedure:

1. Bring an object to class that you can eat or drink.

2. Put students into small groups and they have to think of a few words for each of the senses related to that object (see, smell, feel, hear, taste).

3. At the end of the allotted time, each group can share a few of their most interesting words with the class.

4. Do another round with a different object if you'd like. Or, make it a regular warmer activity.

20 Questions

Skills: Speaking/listening

Time: 5-15 minutes

This is a "20 Questions" style game that can be based on any topic (animals, jobs, etc.), or you may want to leave it open to any person, place, or thing. It's ideal for helping students work on yes/no questions and answers.

If you choose to limit it to a narrower category such as jobs, make it into a "10 Questions" game because it may be too easy with 20.

Remember to maximize student talking time, so only play this game with the entire class if there are fewer than ten students. More than that and students can play in groups of 4-6.

To start off, the teacher thinks of a secret thing in the appropriate category. In groups of 2-3, the students ask the teacher a yes/no question and the teacher answers. Or, they can make a guess at the secret thing. Either way, it counts as one question.

Then, students can take turns being the one with the "secret." This is better because it's more student centered. Students have to listen well instead of just focusing on asking the questions. I usually make the student quickly tell me their secret thing so that I can assist if necessary and keep the game on track. Plus, you'll want to make sure that students have not chosen some obscure thing that their classmates don't know!

Overall, it's an excellent way for students to practice asking questions in English. Just be sure that students are making sentences and not saying something like, "Big?" I assist with this by writing examples of yes/no questions on the board. If we're playing together as a class, I won't answer the question until a complete sentence is made. If students are playing in smaller groups, I circulate during the activity and provide gentle correction about making sentences.

Teaching Tips:

I use a few rules that make things go more smoothly:

1. A guess counts as a "question." This prevents random guessing which can be quite boring.

2. The team or person must use a full sentence to ask a question. The questions have to be yes/no type.

3. For children, emphasize that they must tell the truth at all times! Also, they should choose something that everyone knows, instead of some obscure, random thing. I will usually get them to tell me their secret thing first in order to prevent any problems with this.

Procedure:

1. Choose a secret person, place or thing. Or, have a student do this. You may want to limit it to a certain area for beginners such as jobs or animals.

2. Students take turns asking yes/no questions using complete sentences. The teacher or student with the secret thing in mind answers yes or no. Or, students can also make a guess at the answer which counts as a question.

3. The game continues until students have guessed the correct answer or have run out of questions. You can play more rounds as time allows. Each round usually takes around five minutes.

120-90-60

Skills: Speaking/listening

Time: 15 minutes

Give students a topic that they know a lot about. For example: good or bad points about their school or hometown. I often give half the students one topic and the other half another just to make it a bit more interesting to listen to. Give students 3-5 minutes to prepare, depending on their level. But, emphasize that they should just write one or two words for each point, and not full sentences because it's a speaking activity, not a writing one.

Then, with a partner, the first student has to give their speech and talk continuously for two minutes, while their partner listens. I use an online stopwatch so that the students can see the clock count down. Then, I give the students another two minutes and they switch roles.

After that, the students have to find a new partner and the activity repeats, except they have to include ALL the same information as before, just in 90 seconds. Then, switch again, with 60 more seconds. One way that you can help students make the transition to less time is by giving them 30 seconds between rounds to think about how to say something more concisely, go over in their head the part of their speech where they had to slow down for some reason or to think about where they could use conjunctions.

For lower level students, you can adjust the times to make them shorter and easier because talking for two minutes can be quite difficult.

Emphasize that students must include all of the key information even though they have less time to say it. Speak more quickly or more concisely!

Teaching Tips:

It can be difficult to find good speaking activities that are focused on fluency instead of accuracy, but this is an excellent one and I try to use it a couple of times per semester.

Emphasize to students that they must include all the same information they spoke the first time, so they'll either have to say things more concisely or speak faster. Present it as a difficult, but attainable challenge that they can achieve. At the end of the second and third rounds, ask students how much they were able to include as a percentage. If they did well, tell them to pat themselves on the back for achieving something that wasn't easy. A small motivational moment in your class!

It's a good idea to remind students that spoken speech is more informal than written discourse, particularly in the areas of sentence length and connectors. When we write, things like "however," "although," and "moreover" are common but in spoken speech we mostly just use simple connectors like "and," "but," and "or." Also, in spoken discourse the length of an utterance is much shorter and we don't need to use complicated grammatical constructions.

Procedure:

1. Give students a topic and some time to prepare their "speech."

2. Students give their speech to a partner, talking for two minutes without stopping. Switch roles and the second student gives their speech.

3. Students find a new partner and give their speech again, this time in 90 seconds. Switch roles.

4. Students find a new partner and give their speech again in 60 seconds. Switch roles.

Association

Skills: Writing/reading/listening

Time: 20+ minutes

A fun way to get students writing is this "association game." Think of a number of words related to a certain theme. For example, the theme of travel could use the following words: holidays, relax, vacation, transportation, food, etc.

You can say these words one by one and students have to write down the first word that comes to mind when you say it. Using the list from above, they might write: Thailand, beach, fun, motorcycle, curry.

When this is done, students can write a story using the words they've thought of. It may or may not be a true story, but it doesn't matter either way. To make it more fun, I require that students must use every word they wrote down once! Of course, allow some time for proofreading and editing before sharing the story with other students.

At the end, you can have students share their stories with another student (larger classes), or with everyone for smaller classes.

Procedure:

1. Think of at least 5-10 words related to a certain theme or topic.

2. Say the words one by one and students have to write down the first word that comes to mind.

3. Using these words, students have to write a story. It can be true or not true. Finally, have students share their story with another student or with the class.

Board or Card Games

Skills: Listening/reading/speaking

Time: 20+ minutes (depends on the game chosen)

Keeping games in a safe and locked place (if students discover it, they may damage or lose pieces, etc.) at school can be a life saver! If you are sick, having a personal emergency but cannot take a day off, or given a mission impossible last second notice that you must teach a class that you cannot prepare for—this emergency resource will be invaluable.

I know that this isn't a "no materials" activity, but if you invest in a few of these resources, you can use them over several years for entire class periods with absolutely no planning required! They'll likely come in handy for a variety of situations. Plus, students enjoy playing them.

Classics like *Monopoly, Snakes & Ladders, Checkers, Life,* or *Scrabble* work well because the students often know how to play them already. However, also try out newer ones like *King of Tokyo* or *Settlers of Catan* with high school students or adults. Card games like *Monopoly Deal, Skip-Bo, Uno* or *Phase 10* are always popular with students too.

Once you invest in a few of these games, you'll wonder how you ever lived without them! There's almost nothing else that can fill an entire hour of class time with such a little amount of effort from the teacher in terms of preparation. By little effort, I mean zero! There are certainly times when this is exactly what you need for whatever emergency thing may have come up at your school or in your personal life.

Boggle

Skill: Writing

Time: 10 minutes

You've probably played the word game Boggle before. Shake up the letters and then you have a certain amount of time to make some words with connecting letters. It's possible to play with students and you don't need the actual Boggle game.

Make up a grid on the whiteboard, PowerPoint or on a piece of paper. It only takes a minute to do this. It's possible to do it on the spot if you go with the whiteboard option.

I make a 6x6 grid and put some obvious words in like the names of colors or animals, or the vocabulary that I've recently been teaching. Then, students divide into pairs and they have to make as many words as possible that are 4+ letters. You can give a bonus for longer words if you like. For example, they get two points instead of one if their word is six letters or more.

I always point out to my students to make good use of the "S." They can essentially get two words instead of one by using it. For example:

- fire, fires, mane, manes, fate, fates

This will help the groups who figure this out from running away with the game when other groups have not!

At the end, students count up how many points they have. Double-check for any errors and then award a small prize to the winning team. Depending on class size and how much time you have, you can check the answers of the top 1-2 teams who will get a prize or the entire class.

Procedure:

1. Prepare a "Boggle" grid. The no preparation way is to draw it on the whiteboard.

2. Students divide into pairs and try to make as many words as possible with 4+

letters. Students cannot use/repeat the same letter in a single square within a single word.

3. Students add up points. The teacher checks the answers of all the teams, or only the top teams who will get a prize.

o	r	p	t	s	a
e	a	i	e	t	f
b	k	n	e	r	i
a	d	r	g	o	r
c	o	t	l	s	e
k	f	h	m	a	n

Some possible words from this board:

g reen, pink, rake, back, fire, fires, fast, road, rose, mane, manes (there are many others)

Bucket Lists

Skills: Writing/speaking

Time: 5-10 minutes

Write a sample bucket list on the whiteboard and do a demonstration of how to talk about a bucket list. Give students about five minutes to create a list of three things they want to do, see, or accomplish before they die. Have them partner up to discuss their three wishes for 2-3 minutes, then change partners.

Procedure:

1. Ask students if they have heard the term "bucket list." Then, tell them three things you want to do, see, or accomplish before you die.

2. Give students about five minutes to create their own bucket lists.

3. Divide students into partners to share their bucket lists, then have them change partners. Encourage students to ask each other some follow-up questions.

Cocktail Party

Skills: Speaking/listening

Time: 10-15 minutes

Small talk is a necessary skill, but can be difficult for non-native speakers, especially those from countries where such conversation is not common. Explain to the students that they are at a cocktail party being thrown by their spouse/partner's company. They must engage in small talk with a group of 3-4 people for 2-3 minutes. Scaffold the activity by explaining some common cocktail party conversation topics: current events, sports, even the weather, if they must. Let them know certain topics are typically NOT appropriate at a cocktail party: political opinions, religious discussions, salary, or any other controversial topics. Additionally, demonstrate how to ask follow-up questions.

The main points of the activity are to practice speaking with relative strangers about inconsequential topics and asking follow-up questions. Wrap up the activity by asking each group what topics they discussed and give feedback.

Teaching Tip:

Depending on the level, when you demonstrate the activity, you may need to bring to their attention that you are making follow-up questions based on your partner's answers. Otherwise, students may end up asking each other a list of unrelated questions without listening to the answers.

Procedure:

1. Explain to your class that they will be attending a cocktail party for their spouse/partner's company. Their spouse/partner is called away from them (to answer a call, talk to the boss, whatever), so they must mingle alone.

2. Elicit from students typical topics of cocktail party conversation. Add to the list, as necessary: current events, sports, favorite TV shows (particularly very popular ones that the other guests are likely to be familiar with), etc.

3. Elicit from students topics of conversation which would NOT be appropriate, such as salary, age, religion, etc. If necessary, explain that these topics would be considered too personal or controversial for a cocktail party.

4. Have students stand and begin to mingle.

5. After 2-3 minutes, have students change groups. Time allowing, have them chat in three groups for 2-3 minutes each.

Complaint Desk

Skills: Speaking/listening

Time: 10+ minutes

Complaining, apologizing, and customer service vary from country to country, so students may not know how to complain in English. In this role play, students will take turns complaining to a customer service desk and being the representative dealing with the complaints. Give them a scenario, including the type of business and reason for the complaint, or you can have them brainstorm their own.

Begin the lesson with some useful vocabulary, such as:

- Excuse me,

- I'm sorry, but…

- Would you mind…?

- How can I help you?

- What exactly is the problem?

- I'm terribly/so sorry (to hear that.)

- To make up for this…

Then, divide students into pairs. If you are not giving them a scenario, give them 2-3 minutes to brainstorm a time when they had a customer service complaint. You may want to make some suggestions, such as defective merchandise, a disappointing meal, or an incorrect bill. Have the pairs then take turns being the customer and being the employee.

Teaching Tip:

For higher-level students, encourage a bit more creativity: try to negotiate a lower bill, or (as customer service) give reasons to deny their request, for example.

Procedure:

1. Begin class with an introduction on complaining and apologizing in English and useful vocabulary for making a complaint to customer service.

2. Divide students into pairs. Give them a scenario, or 2-3 minutes to brainstorm their own.

3. Have students take turns being the customer and the customer service representative.

Conversation Topic

Skills: Speaking/listening

Time: 10 minutes

Give students a topic. They will generate questions to ask each other and have a small conversation.

Teaching Tip:

Remind students that it is more important to listen and respond to each other than to just run through their list of questions. The time given to think of several questions should simply prepare them to speak about the topic with fewer pauses.

Procedure:

1. Divide students into groups of 3-5.

2. Give them a topic from current events or popular culture, etc. and 1-2 minutes to generate 2-3 questions to ask each other.

3. Give them 5 minutes to ask and answer each other's questions.

Deserted Island

Skills: Listening/writing/speaking

Time: 10-15 minutes

Deserted Island is an excellent way to uncover what things are most important to students. Tell students that there is a terrible storm and their ship is sinking, but thankfully, they can bring three objects with them. It doesn't need to be realistic or necessary for survival, just something that they want to have with them during their time on the island. Encourage creativity and imagination.

Do this activity by having students say their answers out loud. But, if you want to focus on writing, they can write down three things, along with the reasons why they chose those items. It can be done individually, or in a group.

Procedure:

1. Tell students that they are on a ship and it's sinking. Thankfully, there is an island nearby that is already well-stocked with everything they'll need for survival.

2. Each student (or group) has to choose three things that they'd like to have with them during their time on the island. It doesn't need to be realistic or necessary for survival.

3. Students write down their answers and reasons why. They can share them with a small group or the class when they're done. Depending on the level, it takes most students around five minutes to think of their objects, and then five more minutes to share with a group.

Draw an Idiom

Skills: Listening/reading/speaking

Time: 10-20 minutes

Give students an idiom and have them draw a picture of the idiom. Then, have them share their drawings and elicit possible meanings. Finish by giving them the actual meaning and several example sentences to write in their notebooks.

Procedure:

1. Give students an idiom, such as "raining cats and dogs" and give them 3 minutes draw a representative picture.

2. When time is up, have students share their pictures and elicit guesses about what the idiom may mean before telling students the actual meaning.

3. Finish the activity by giving students several example sentences or scenarios using the idiom for them to write in their notebooks.

Fortunately, Unfortunately / Luckily, Unluckily

Skills: Speaking/listening

Time: 5-10 minutes

You may have played this game at school yourself. Start of by telling students some good news (something that "happened to you") followed by some bad news. For example, "Unfortunately, my car wouldn't start this morning. Fortunately, my neighbor gave me a ride to school. Unfortunately, she drove through a red light. Fortunately..." Students will then generate similar language using fortunately/unfortunately or luckily/unluckily.

Procedure:

1. Divide students into small groups of 3-5.

2. Give them a scenario (something that "happened to you"), alternating between good and bad news. For example, "Unfortunately, my car wouldn't start this morning. Fortunately, my neighbor gave me a ride to school. Unfortunately, she drove through a red light. Fortunately..."

3. Have students take turns within their groups adding one element at a time. Each

addition should change the story from good to bad or vice versa.

4. Give students a time limit (5 minutes or so) or have them take 2-3 turns around the circle.

Freeze

Skills: Writing/reading/listening

Time: 5-20 minutes

This is a group writing activity that you can have a lot of fun with. The way it works is that you think of a story starter. For example, "Tom decided to _____." Students have to start the story off, and after 30 seconds or a minute, you can say, "Freeze."

Then, students pass their paper one to the right/behind/etc., depending on how the classroom is arranged. That student has to read the story and then continue it. You can repeat the freeze and pass as many times as you like, but I usually give a warning when it's the last round so students can finish up the story.

Read the stories out loud to the class and see which one is the best.

Procedure:

1. Write a story starter on the board. For example, "Amy had a terrible day! She _____."

2. Each student has to continue the story for 30 seconds to 1 minute. Then say, "Freeze!"

3. Students pass their paper in an organized fashion and continue the story. Repeat as many times as you like, but warn students when it's the last round so they can finish it off.

4. Read the stories out loud with the class.

Group Therapy

Skills: Speaking/listening

Time: 10-15 minutes

In the style of an AA meeting, students sit in a circle if possible and introduce themselves, "My name is _____, and I'm _____." Instead of finishing with ". . . and I'm an alcoholic," finish with a problem they have learning English, such as using articles correctly or conjugating verbs. They should then solicit tips and tricks from their classmates.

The teacher should begin by modeling and could give an actual problem they have as a language student. For example, "My name is Jennifer, and I'm never sure how formal or polite to be when speaking Korean to someone I don't know well. Does anyone have any advice for me?"

Procedure:

1. Before class, arrange the desks in a circle, if possible. If the class is very large, divide students into several large groups.

2. Begin by telling students that everyone has trouble learning languages, and even those who speak several languages fluently have difficulty with some aspect of any language they learn.

3. Introduce the lesson as "therapy" for them to get counseling for their troubles.

4. Begin with your own example of a problem you have with a foreign language you speak. For example, "My name is Jennifer, and I'm never sure how formal or polite to be when speaking Korean to someone I don't know well. Does anyone have any advice for me?"

5. Go around the circle and give each student a turn to introduce themselves, "My name is _____, and I'm _____." Instead of finishing with ". . . and I'm an alcoholic," finish with a problem they have learning English, such as using articles correctly or conjugating verbs. They should then solicit tips and tricks from their classmates.

I'm Going on a Picnic

Skills: Listening/speaking

Time: 5-10 minutes

This is an oldie, but a goodie. It gets students talking and thinking critically. Think of a rule for items on the picnic, but don't tell the class. For example, "must contain the letter E," or, "must be a countable noun." Tell them you are going on a picnic and give examples of 3-5 items you are taking with you to give them hints about your rule. Then, elicit from the students what they would take. If their item doesn't fit your rule, tell them they can't take it and that they can't come with you!

To keep wait times between turns shorter, have large classes work in groups of 2-3, rather than individually. In any case, set a time limit for each person or group making a guess (20-30 seconds), or they are out. The group to guess the rule wins.

Please note that groups are not out if they suggest an item that doesn't match the rule, or if they guess the wrong rule. The time limit is to keep the game moving and disqualifying students for not making guesses keeps students from just listening to other guesses to guess the rule without otherwise contributing.

Procedure:

1. Think of a rule for items which can go on the picnic, such as "must contain the letter E," or, "must be countable."

2. Tell the class you are going on a picnic and give examples of 3-5 items you are taking with you to give them hints about your rule.

3. Elicit from the students what they would take. If their item doesn't fit your rule, tell them they can't take it.

4. Have large classes work in groups of 2-3 and set a 20-30 second time limit to keep wait times between turns shorter. The group to guess the rule wins.

Interesting Story and Questions

Skills: Writing/reading/speaking/listening

Time: 10-30 minutes

Have students write something interesting. Some examples are: most embarrassing moment, scariest thing you've ever done, your dream for the future, etc. Base it on whatever you are teaching in class. Then, distribute the stories to other people in the class. They have to go around the class, finding the person whose story they have by asking questions. Once they find that person, they have to ask three interesting questions about the story.

Teaching Tips:

Emphasize to students that they are to practice asking good *full-sentence* questions. For example, "USA?" is not a good question, while, "Did you study abroad in the USA?" is much better. Also emphasize that students should think of interesting follow-up questions that expand upon their knowledge about that situation. This involves reading carefully so they can avoid asking about things that are already mentioned. Give students a couple of minutes before the activity starts to write down a few questions based on the paper they received to help facilitate this.

This activity provides an excellent opportunity for students to work on reported speech. This is something that high level students are often surprisingly weak at. With a small class (fewer than 10), students can report what they learned about their partner to everyone. If larger, students can tell their seating partner what they learned. For example, students might say something like, "I talked to Min-Ji. She told me that she got in a car accident last year. She said that it was scary, but thankfully nobody got injured seriously. "

Procedure:

1. Have students write an interesting story based on a certain topic. Adjust for length and difficulty.

2. Collect stories and redistribute them—one per student, making sure a student does not get their own story.

3. Students go around the class asking people if they have their story. For example, "Did you get in a car accident when you were little?"

4. When they find the person, they must ask them three interesting follow-up questions about it.

5. Do the optional variation of having students tell other people what they learned in order to practice using reported speech.

Just a Minute

Skills: Speaking/listening

Time: 5-10 minutes

Materials Required: Whiteboard, timer (cellphone)

This is a very simple activity that you can use as a fast warm-up at the beginning of class in order to get students talking and giving a very informal speech about a certain topic. Write a bunch of general categories on the board such as jobs, hobbies, dreams, movies, food, etc. Put the students into groups of 4 and they can number themselves 1-2-3-4.

Then, ask one of the students to throw a paper airplane at the board and whatever word it gets closest to is the topic for the first student. All the number ones must talk about that topic for one minute without stopping and if they stop or have a long pause of more than three seconds, they've lost the challenge. You can adjust the time limit to be higher or lower depending on the level of students (beginner = 30 seconds, advanced = 2 minutes).

Erase the first speaking round word from the board and continue the activity with the remaining three students except that they have different topics. It's helpful if the teacher does an example first with a topic that the students choose.

Teaching Tip:

For higher level students, you can require that their teammates listen carefully and each of them has to ask the speaker an *interesting* follow-up question or two.

Procedure:

1. The teacher writes topics on the whiteboard (teacher-supplied, or elicited from students).

2. Put students into groups of 4. They number themselves 1-2-3-4.

3. The teacher does an example speech with a topic that students choose.

4. One student throws a paper airplane at the whiteboard. The topic closest to where it hits is the first one.

5. Student one has to talk about that topic for a minute without stopping. The goal is to have minimal pauses and to never stop talking. (Optional: the other three students each ask a follow-up question).

6. Erase the first speaking round word. Another student throws the paper airplane and finds a different topic. The number two student talks for a minute. Continue with the third and fourth rounds' students.

Never Have I Ever

Skills: Speaking/listening

Time: 10-20 minutes

Students think of a few things that they haven't done but that they think others in the class have. For example, maybe someone hasn't been to China but most of the people in the class probably have. Or, someone has never tried Indian or Vietnamese food.

The first student starts with one of their statements, saying, "Never have I ever _____." The other students listen and if they have done it, they get a point. I usually get students to keep track of points themselves by writing a tick on their paper or in their notebook. If you have a small class, you can appoint a captain to do this on the board. You go around the room until everyone has said at least one statement (for big classes) or a couple of them (smaller classes) and then tally up the final points. Whoever has the most points is the "winner" and the person who has had the most interesting life so far! If you have a large class, it's best to divide students up into groups of 7-10.

Teaching Tips:

This game is quite difficult to explain, even to people who speak English as their first language so doing a demonstration with multiple examples is vital.

Procedure:

1. Give students time to prepare 2-3 statements; the amount of time depends on the level of students. They need to think of things that they've never done, but which they think their classmates have.

2. The first student says one of their statements. If someone else has done it, they put up their hand to signify this and they get one point. I usually have students keep track of the points themselves or appoint a captain to do this.

3. The next person can say their statement and you follow the same procedure, until everyone has said at least one statement. You can also continue until you've done two or three rounds, depending on your class size.

4. The person with the most points has had the most interesting life.

Practice Writing Fluently

Skill: Writing

Time: 5-10 minutes/class

For speaking and writing, there are two main ways to evaluate it: fluency and accuracy. Fluency is how fast you are able to do it. Accuracy is how good your grammar and vocabulary are. It's more complicated than that, but that's the simple explanation!

Most English writing classes and textbooks focus on accuracy. It's much easier for a book, or teacher to point out grammar and vocab errors than to teach you to write quickly. However, it's important to work on both.

Each student needs a notebook that they'll use only for this purpose. Assign students a topic for each class they will do the fluency writing practice in. For example, "My family," or, "Plans for the weekend," or, "Hopes for the future," or, "My favourite book." Then, have them write about that topic for five minutes (or ten once they get used to it) without using a cell-phone and dictionary. Beginners may only be able to do it for three minutes. The goal is to write quickly. If students don't know how to spell something, just guess. It doesn't matter in a fluency writing exercise.

This is the most important thing—the pen should NEVER stop moving. If they can't think of anything, write this sentence, "I don't know what to write. I don't know what to write. I don't. . ." After two or three times, they'll think of something else! If you see a student not writing, tell them to make sure that their pen doesn't stop moving.

Over time, you'll notice that the amount they can write increases! Remember that the goal is to write more quickly, not to write accurately. Students can work on grammar, vocabulary and structure at other times.

Procedure:

1. Students get a notebook specifically for fluent writing practice.

2. Assign a topic of the day and amount of time to write.

3. Students write for that specified amount of time without a cell-phone or dictionary. The goal is to write quickly.

4. Pens should never stop moving! Students can write, "I don't know what to write" instead.

5. Track progress over time with a word count chart.

Round Robin Story

Skills: Listening/speaking

Time: 10 minutes

This activity is easy, low prep, and doesn't require any materials. To begin, have the students sit in a large circle. Start them off with a "Once upon a time _____" sentence. Say it as well as write it on the whiteboard.

The story then builds as it travels around the room. Each student adds one sentence, which you write (with any mistakes corrected) on the board. This is not a memory game—students only need to add a new sentence which continues the story, rather than repeat it from the beginning. It should, however, make sense in the context of the story.

When all students have added a sentence, you can either add a sentence to end it, if necessary, or ask for volunteers to finish the story. Then, the entire class can read the story aloud from the board. If you have not written it on the board, you can retell or summarize it.

As far as content goes, it should obviously be appropriate for a classroom but I try not to censor it unless it's quite bad. After all, it's their story, not mine! Another situation I've had is where students recreate a typical Disney story for example. I view this as not a bad thing as long as they're using English to do it. Plus, there's usually one student in the class who likes to throw a bit of a twist into the plot to make things interesting.

Teaching Tips:

For more active participation (and if necessary to prompt/help students), you may want to ask students open-ended questions about the story while it is still being written. Even if they have to refer to the board, the students will be more actively engaged in the story. This should also help each contribution move the story forward, especially if you are getting a lot of descriptive sentences without much plot.

If your class is large, this will take longer than 5-10 minutes if all students contribute. You could randomly choose students to contribute until time is up, or plan on a longer activity.

Another option for a larger class is to put students into smaller groups of four and have them write their story down, passing it from person to person for each sentence. I suggest ringing a bell every 60-90 seconds to switch papers to keep things moving along nicely. To make things more interesting, grab a paper randomly if someone finishes before the time is up and add a fun sentence to it! You could even keep some papers with story starters in your emergency teaching kit or the back of your attendance folder for this activity.

Procedure:

1. Have students sit in a large circle, if possible. Begin with a "Once upon a time" sentence. Say it and write it on the whiteboard.

2. Have the student closest to you add a sentence and the teacher writes it (correctly) on the board.

3. Continue around the room, until everyone has added a sentence or two.

4. Add a sentence to end the story, or have volunteers finish it.

5. Have a student (or several) read the complete story to the class. If you have not written it, summarize or retell it.

Secret Person

Skills: Writing/reading/speaking/listening

Time: 15-30 minutes

This is the perfect activity for using "be" statements in the past tense. Have students think of two dead people and write down their details: when they were born, where they were from, why they were famous, how they died, and one or two more interesting things.

Then, put the students into small groups of 4-5 to play together. The first student gives the student to the right of them the first hint and they get one guess. If correct that student gets a point and goes next, starting with the person on their right. If incorrect, the first student gives the next hint to the next person to the right and they get a guess. This pattern continues until the correct answer is guessed.

Teaching Tips:

It's possible to play this game with the whole class, but it's better in small groups because it's far more student-centered. Of course, do a demonstration first with the whole class before you let them play together.

Many students pick the same two or three people, depending on the country where you are teaching. I avoid this situation by using those people as my examples. I'll say something like, "You need to pick two dead people, for example, Michael Jackson and Kim Jong II." In Korea, a couple more people you could ban are Lee Sun Shin and King Sejong!

Procedure:

1. Do a demonstration for the students first. Think of a dead person. Give some hints, such as when he was born, where he was from, why he was famous, etc.

2. Have the students guess who the person is after each hint.

3. Put students into small groups and have them choose two dead people and write some hints about him/her. Giving around 5-6 hints is best. Be sure to start with the hardest ones and get to the easiest ones at the end.

4. The students do rock-scissors-paper and the winner goes first. She gives the person to her right the most difficult hint and then that person gets one guess. If

correct, he gets a point and the game continues with his secret person. He starts with the person on his right. If incorrect, she gives the next student to the right in the circle the next hint and they get one guess. It continues until the correct guess is given.

Talk Show

Skills: Speaking/listening

Time: 15 minutes

This is a pair work variation of self-introductions. My higher level students tend to find this more fun than the same old self-introductions they do all the time. I set up the front of the class as a talk show set with a desk and chair (for the host) and a chair for the person being interviewed. Then, I divide the students into pairs. Before beginning, I introduce the activity by asking students about talk shows. Most students will be very familiar with the concept. We then discuss what kinds of questions a host might ask.

One pair at a time comes to the front and the two students take turns being the host and the guest. The host is given either a set number of questions to ask or a time limit. After each host's time is up, the teacher can open the floor to "audience" questions.

Teaching Tips:

While introducing the topic, it may be helpful to brainstorm a written list of questions on the white board for them to refer to as needed. However, you will need to remind them that talk show hosts look at the person as they ask questions.

The larger the class, the less time each pair will have to speak in front of the class. So, if your class is very large, limit each pair to 2-3 questions each before switching roles. If you have a large class and a short period, this may not be a feasible activity for even an entire class period.

Procedure:

1. Before class, set up a desk and chair and another chair, similar to the set-up of a talk-show.

2. To demonstrate, show the class a short clip of a popular celebrity being interviewed on a talk show to show the class, or simply talk about talk shows: what kinds of questions are asked, etc.

3. Divide students into pairs: interviewer/host and guest. (They will switch roles.)

4. Have one pair at time come to the front of the class (the audience) and conduct their interviews. The guests are playing themselves—this is a self-introduction.

5. After a set number of questions (about 5) or your time limit, allow questions to be asked by the audience. Then, have the students switch roles.

The "Expert" Conversation Activity

Skills: Speaking/listening

Time: 15-30 minutes

Students write down five things that they're an expert in. Once they've written their lists, they circle the three that they think will be most interesting to other students in the class. Next, divide the students up into pairs and give them about 5-6 minutes to ask some questions to their partner about things they are experts in. Keep changing partners for as long as you want the activity to last, but more than 3-4 times gets kind of boring.

Teaching Tips:

This is a particularly useful activity for practicing many of the speaking sub-skills such as initiating a conversation, turn-taking, and appropriate length of responses. You can pre-teach some of these things before you begin the activity. For example, show students how to initiate a conversation by saying something like, "I see you're interested in _____. What/where/why/when/who/how _____?"

Teach students about appropriate length of responses by doing one bad example and then one good example. Continue with the bad example by rambling on and on until the students are feeling a little bit uncomfortable and they'll see clearly what you mean.

If possible, try to get students to talk to someone that they don't know. This is particularly helpful for the students who don't know anybody else in the class, or don't have a friend. Having a five minute conversation with someone makes you feel like you know them and these students won't be so alone in future classes. I do this by asking students to choose partners whose names they don't know.

Procedure:

1. Talk about what "expert" means. Tell them five things that you're an expert in.
2. Students make a list of 5 items.
3. Students choose the three things that they think will be most interesting to the others in the class. Tell students to do the same with their own lists.
4. Students find a partner and talk together for 5-6 minutes about the chosen topics. Starting the conversation, turn-taking and changing topics is up to them.
5. Students switch partners and continue.

What Can I do with a _____?

Skills: Speaking/listening

Time: 5-10 minutes

Show students some random common object (potatoes are often used for this activity, but I like to use some kind of "trash" to introduce a lesson on recycling.) Have students work as a class or in small groups to brainstorm as many possible uses for the item as possible. This is a fun way to get some creative juices flowing!

Give them a time limit (3-5 minutes), then discuss their answers. If some answers seem too outlandish, have the student or group explain how or why they would use the item in that way.

Procedure:

1. In advance, prepare an object. A potato is commonly used, but it can be anything.
2. Divide students into groups of 3-5.
3. Give them 3-5 minutes to brainstorm creative uses for the object.
4. As a class, briefly discuss their various ideas.
5. You can have the class choose the best idea, if you like.

What Do you Know about Apples?

Skill: Writing

Time: 5-10 minutes

In this writing activity, students have to think of all the true statements they know about a certain topic. For example, apples, cats, David Beckham, etc. For apples, students may come up with the following sentences:

- There's an English idiom, "An apple a day keeps the doctor away."

- An apple is a fruit.

- There are green apples.

- There are red apples.

Put students into groups of 3-4 and give them an allotted time (5 minutes). They have to write down all the true sentences they can think of about the topic.

The team with the most sentences is the winner. Of course, check and see that they're correct! You can use the Internet if necessary to confirm things you may be unsure about. For a small class, it may be possible to check all the answers. But, for a larger class, you may just want to check the top 1-2 teams.

Teaching Tip:

Mention to students that they should not write negative statements. For example, "An apple is not a vegetable." Unless you do this, you'll inevitably get one team who writes twenty sentences with, "An apple is not a/an animal/vegetable/car/piece of clothing."

Procedure:

1. Put students into groups of 3-4. Give them a topic (apples).

2. Students have to write as many true, positive statements as they can.

3. The winner is the team with the most true sentences at the end of the allotted time.

What did you Do this Weekend?

Skills: Writing/listening/speaking

Time: 10-15 minutes

On a piece of paper, each student writes down three things they did this past weekend. They must be true. For example:

- I slept a lot because I was so tired from work.

- I went to my son's soccer game.

- I cooked a roast beef dinner.

Then, collect all the papers and read them out to the class in random order. They must guess whose paper it is. The class can give opinions on that person's weekend. For example: boring, fun, relaxing, they got a lot accomplished, etc.

Procedure:

1. Students write down three true sentences about their past weekend on a piece of paper.
2. Read out the sentences to the class.
3. Students have to guess whose weekend you are describing. Then, they can give their opinion about what their classmate's weekend was like.
4. (Optional) Ask a follow-up question based on what the student wrote.

Word Poem/Name Poem

Skill: Writing

Time: 15+ minutes

Here is another activity that you undoubtedly did yourself as a student. Either give students a word related to the lesson, or have them use their names (a great ice breaker activity, too!) They simply begin each line with a letter from the word, so that the first letter of each line read vertically spells the word. Using that letter, write a word or phrase that describes the word.

Here's an example word poem: www.eslspeaking.org/word-poem.

Teaching Tip:

These are great for decorating the classroom or including in student portfolios. So, have them make a final draft on copy paper and decorate. The final draft can be done as homework.

Procedure:

1. In advance, prepare your own name or word poem to display for students.

2. Show them that the first letter of each line spells a word.

3. Give them a word related to your lesson or have them use their names to make their own poem.

Words in Words

Skill: Writing

Time: 5-10 minutes

You probably did this when you were in school. Give students a word and have them make as many words as possible using the letters in that word. For example: "vacation" = a, on, no, act, action, taco, ant, van, etc. Ggive a point for each word, so that the student with the most words wins, or give more points for longer words. When time is up (about five minutes), show students the possible answers.

Wordles.com has a tool that allows you to type in a word and get the possible words. For vacation, they listed 45 words, some of which I should have thought of myself and some of which are "Scrabble words." Since students will not possibly know all of these words, it is up to you whether you show all the answers or an abridged list.

Procedure:

5. In advance, prepare a long word and write it on the whiteboard or a PowerPoint or give students individual worksheets.

6. Give students a time limit of about five minutes to make words from the letters in the word.

7. To make it a competition, when time is up, give students points for each word and you may wish to give bonus points for longer words.

8. When the activity is finished, show students all of the possible words they could have made. Find them at www.wordles.com.

Before You Go

Before you go, please leave a review wherever you got this book. I appreciate your feedback and it will help other teachers like yourself find this book. My goal is to spread some ESL teaching awesome to the world!

If you can't get enough ESL games, activities and other useful stuff for the classroom in this book, you can get even more goodness delivered straight to your inbox every week. I promise to respect your privacy—your name and email address will never be shared with anyone for any reason.

Printed in Great Britain
by Amazon

50887835R00051